GW01048782

A POCKET GUIDE TO COMMON WILD FLOWERS

Title page:

SILVERWEED *Potentilla anserina*

This is a trailing plant with creeping runners that re-root at intervals.
A damp situation at the roadside or a stony field favours the growth of this perennial yellow-flowered plant. Its long pinnate leaves are covered with a growth of fine hair and the edges of the leaflets are deeply serrated. The attractive five-lobed flowers are borne singly on a long stalk which grows from the axils of the leaves.
Flowering June to August and again in September.

A Pocket Guide to Common

WILD
FLOWERS

Illustrated by:
Michael Stringer

Text by:
John Shillingford

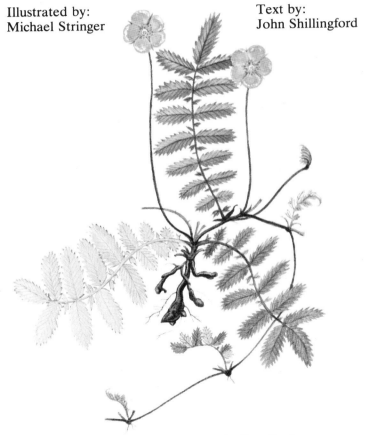

John Bartholomew & Son Ltd.
Edinburgh and London

© This edition 1979
John Bartholomew & Son Ltd.,
12 Duncan Street, Edinburgh, EH9 1TA.
and at 216 High Street, Bromley, BRI 1PW.

ISBN 0 7028 8040 X

Printed in Great Britain

'Lo! when the buds expand, the leaves are green,
then the first opening of the flower is seen;
Then come the rosy breath and humid smile,
That with their sweets the willing sense beguile;
But as we look, and love, and taste, and praise,
And the fruit grows, the charming flower decays;
Till all is gathered, and the wintry blast
Mourns o'er the place of love and pleasure past.'

CRABBE

Introduction

The changes described by the poet are indeed full of interest
and beauty. Few people are so insensible as to be completely
unaware of nature's beauty, and yet too few have had their
minds awakened to the succession of beautiful and varied
form, which year by year adorns our fields and woods, our
rocks and moorlands and even the hedge-sides and ditches.
There are many with ample time and leisure, yet who do not
know even by sight our commonest wild flowers, and yet
there is not one wild flower which does not exhibit a perfec-
tion of structure of awe-inspiring beauty.

There are many thousands of wild flower species and this
book cannot pretend to be more than a fleeting introduction
to the commonest that are found the World over. Neither is
it a botanical work, there are already many of those of
greater use to the inquiring student of botany. This book
shows the basic construction of flowers by means of simple
drawings, coupled with true-to-life colour drawings of some
sixty species. The skill of the artist will bring the flowers to
life for even the 'armchair naturalist'.

Few pursuits can provide such innocent and absorbing study,
than the study of wild flowers generally. Such little equip-
ment is required—a magnifying glass and perhaps a couple of
needles to pry into the depths of flowers is all that is needed.

GOLDEN ROD *Solidago virgaurea*

The Golden Rod's natural habitat is North America where more than eighty different species exist. It is able to thrive in rough sandy ground, where its growth is somewhat stunted but sturdy. In more favourable conditions it can reach a height of 1m. or 1½m. The long narrow spear-shaped leaves have slightly toothed edges and are arranged alternate sides on the straight stems which are covered with a coating of fine downy hairs. These stems carry a number of branches at the top which support a number of yellow flower heads.
Flowering July to September, (Perennial).

Golden Rod

Stone-crop

STONE-CROP
Sedum acre

This perennial has succulent stems and leaves which retain moisture. It grows in the crevices of dry-stone walls and rocks and is sometimes known as Wall Pepper. It is protected from drought by its reserves of water and can survive even out of soil for some time.

The flowers are symmetrical with five or six green sepals and a similar number of yellow petals, and twice that number of stamens, arranged in two rows.

Flowering June to August.

COMMON GORSE
Ulex europaeus

Although common in Britain, Europe and the North-West corner of Africa, the Gorse is rarely found in America or other parts of the World. It is however a delightfully scented plant often found growing near the sea, its scent faithfully carried on a fresh sea breeze.

The Gorse is evergreen, and the flowers can be found blooming at most times of the year. The bright yellow butterfly-shaped blooms are protected by sharp spikes, ready to prick the unwary botanist.

The seed is carried in little pods, which when ripe split with an audible crack and disperse their small black seeds.

Flowering almost all the year round.

Common Gorse

Lesser Celandine

LESSER CELANDINE *Ranunculus ficaria*

This attractive flower carries a golden yellow head with seven to twelve petals and three sepals. It propagates quickly, often forming a dense carpet of dark green leaves and yellow flowers. The fruit is in the form of an achene and carries a solitary seed. This is not a limiting factor to their propagation however, since the roots produce a large number of tubers, each of which can produce a new plant.

The leaves springing from the rootstock are larger than the stem-borne leaves, and are marked with blotches of either a brownish or whitish hue. As the first warm sun appears so the Lesser Celandine puts in an appearance, and remains in bloom until midsummer when the flowers and leaves die back, leaving the tubers in the soil to rise again the following year.

MARSH MARIGOLD *Caltha palustris*

As is obvious from its common name, this delightful bright yellow flower thrives best in wet marshy conditions and is often to be found in marshy meadows or growing beside a sluggish stream or quiet pool.

The green stems grow from a thick creeping rootstock, and they are hollow-designed to carry up the water so necessary for the well-being of the flower. The stems thicken here and there and branch, producing a heart-shaped darkly veined leaf. These branches terminate in a single bright yellow cup-shaped bloom formed from five enlarged sepals. The cup centre has a number of carpels surrounded by a large number of stamens which later develop seed pods.

Flowering March to July.

Marsh Marigold

Coltsfoot

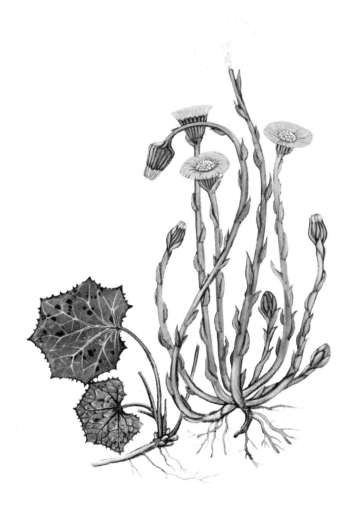

COLTSFOOT

Tussilago farfara

A thick perennial rootstock establishes this herb in even the most inhospitable soil, and it is often found growing on railway embankments. It is a peculiar plant, in that the flowers appear before the leaves.

The flower stems are hard, thick and hollow and are sheathed at intervals with furry bracts arranged in a spiral. The flowers are carried singly and are composed of several rings of fine strap-shaped rays, while in the centre is a mass of tube-shaped florets. The bloom has a surround of narrow green leaves which in turn are surrounded by the sheathing bracts of the stem.

The flowers are succeeded by soft downy heads similar but not as white or dainty as those of the Dandelion. Each are composed of scores of seeds which are wafted away on the breeze, some of which produce new plants and some of which are stolen by birds to line their nests. After the seeds have taken to the wind the second part of the Coltsfoot's life begins, and large, broadly heart-shaped green leaves covered with a soft down appear; the down on the upper surface is soon rubbed away leaving the upper surfaces bare, but the undersides clad in the softest down. There is a special reason for this down, as it prevents moisture clogging the evaporation pores on their undersides. This is particularly important on the clay soils in which the Coltsfoot thrives.

Blackberry or Bramble

BLACKBERRY or BRAMBLE

Rubus fruticosus

Many different species of Bramble have been identified, the common bramble grows from a perennial rootstock and has strong and extremely prickly stems.

The white flowers with their five petals are in clusters at the ends of the stems and are followed by the edible fruits which are formed from clusters of pips surrounded by a fleshy sweet fruit.

The leaves are beautifully coloured, in autumn their glowing reds contrasting with their surroundings. Their faces are smooth whilst their backs are coated with hairs.

Flowering June to October.

Cuckoo Pint

CUCKOO PINT

Arum maculatum

This exotic looking plant rises from a tuberous rootstock from which the triangular leaves grow. The leaves are usually speckled with fuzzy black or purple spots. The flower stalk grows from the centre of the leaves and carries a large bract leaf which unfurls to reveal a purple cigar-shaped column, around the base of which are to be found numerous small flowers. The hooded cover called the spathe later withers along with the cigar-shaped cylinder (spadix) but the ovaries evolve into scarlet berries which are carried on a short stem.

HERB ROBERT

Geranium robertianum

The little pink flowers can be found in roadside hedges and woodland clearings, and it can grow on bare and stony soil. It grows about 30cm. high and the dainty flowers are carried on thin branched stems. The leaves are composed of three leaflets each with deeply lobed edges. The foliage starts green, but later changes to a reddish tinge.

The flowers conform to the geranium type—there being a calyx of five separate sepals, a corolla of five separate petals longer than the sepals, plus two rings each composed of five stamens.

The seeds are ejected from the capsules when ripe, spreading over a wide area.

Flowering May, June.

Herb Robert

Rose Bay Willow Herb

ROSE BAY WILLOW HERB

Chamaenerion angustifolium

Another attractive flower that prefers a light, moist soil. The perennial spreading rhizome sends up straight, smooth stems which terminate in racemes of reddish purple flowers. Each flower has four petals, four sepals and eight drooping stamens, four of which are shorter than the others. The flower stalk is in fact the ovary and, after fertilisation, enlarges into a long narrow capsule which splits to reveal the small oval seeds. The leaves are narrow and pointed and grow alternately on the stems on short stalks.
Flowering July to August.

HOGWEED

Heracleum sphondylium

This large plant prefers a moist situation and has a tough, hairy and hollow stem growing some 2m. high. The lower pinnate leaves are very large but they decrease in size further up the stem. The flower head consists of a large number of small stems forming an umbel of pink or white flowers. The flowers on the perimeter of the umbel tend to be larger than the inner ones and more irregular in form.

Hogweed

COMMON TEASEL   *Dipsacus fullonum*

Often to be found on waste-ground and woodland, this biennial herb has a preference for a clay soil. During the first
season it does not produce its prickly head, but consists only
of the leaves that form a flat ground rosette more than 30cm.
across. During the second year thick, spiky stems appear and
grow up to a height of 2m., and these angular stems are
topped by prickly purple heads.

The leaves, where they join the stem, are cup-shaped and
hold rain-water and act as a trap for the unwary insect.
Flowering August and September.

Common Teasel

DAISY

Bellis perennis

This perennial wild flower can be found practically all the year round and is among the commonest of all wild flowers. The vertical rootstock is 15cm. to 20cm. long and produces a rosette of oval-shaped leaves. The flower head is carried on a short stem and consists of about twenty white flat florets which surround the central yellow tubular florets. The outer white ray florets curl up over the central florets at night and in damp weather, and in doing so fertilise the stigmas by contact with the pollen of the central florets. Beneath the flower is a sheath of green bracts which are covered in white hairs which offer a protection against insects.

The stems and leaves contain an unpleasant sap, which is distasteful to animals, and they are often left in peace to propagate as they will, and unless removed soon take over large areas of grassland.

Daisy

Ivy

IVY
Hedera helix

Often found clothing ancient walls, the Ivy is a strong ever-green perennial climber. The climbing stems have five-lobed leaves, but the flowering stems have simple spear-shaped leaves. The greenish yellow flowers appear at the extremities of the branches and are succeeded by blackish berries. Flowering September to October.

LESSER PERIWINKLE
Vinca minor

The leaves of this pleasant blue flower are evergreen and form pleasant ground cover. In some countries they repre-sent a symbol of immortality. It is a perennial plant with short straight stems which rise from a creeping rootstock. The stems have a habit of rooting from the nodes, where these are in contact with the ground. The flowers are solitary and are produced from the axils of the leaves which are lanceolate and produced in opposite pairs. The dark green leaves are smooth to the touch.

The pale purple-blue flowers are composed of a blue corolla with five lobes forming a tube at their base and enclosing the five stamens which grow in a ring half-way up the tube, and a central ovary. There is occasionally a fruit, which consists of two sac-like structures containing the seeds.

Lesser Periwinkle

Red Clover

RED CLOVER   *Trifolium pratense*

The Red or Purple Clover is a common plant which has also been grown extensively as animal hay. The flower heads stand on erect hairy stems and are acorn-shaped and carry two trifoliate leaves beneath them.

The flowers may be found from May to early September, although the leaves and stems can be found at most moderate seasons. The leaves are large, ovate and are frequently marked with a lighter coloured band which divides the leaf across the centre in a quarter moon shape.

There are about twenty different species of Clover, among the most common of which are the Red Clover, the White Clover *(T. repens)* and the Crimson Clover *(T. incarnatum)*.

COMMON VETCH   *Vicia sativa*

The Common Vetch is sometimes grown as animal fodder. It is a clinging plant that supports itself with its clinging tendrils which wrap around neighbouring plants. It is found in dry pastures and open woods and flowers in spring and early summer.

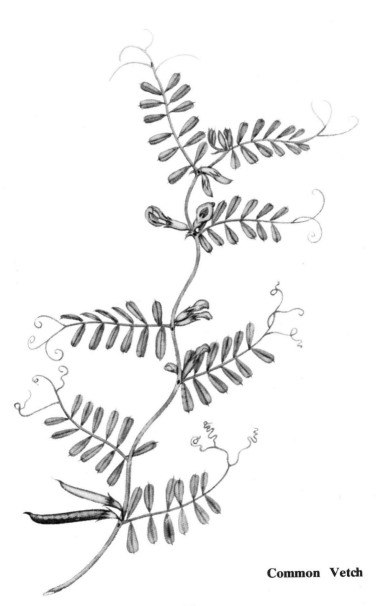

Common Vetch

Sweet Violet

SWEET VIOLET   *Viola odorata*

This lovely spring flower prefers a chalky soil, and is quite
often found growing under hedges and in the borders of
meadows. Broad heart-shaped leaves are carried on long
stems which spring from the rhizome. The flowers form
singly on long stems and vary from reddish-blue, purple to
white. It has a very pleasant scent.
Flowers March to May.

35

Yellow Flag

YELLOW FLAG   *Iris pseudacorus*

Few wild flowers can rival the majestic beauty of this fine flower. It grows well in damp situations, beside ponds and rivers. The erect stems rise from a thick creeping rootstock which grows horizontally in the ground and out of which many little rootlets grow downwards.

The lower leaves are 60cm. or 1m. tall, sharp and sword-shaped, the upper leaves are shorter and grow close to the stem.

The flower head is exotic looking and is formed from three large drooping petal-like sepals of bright yellow with brownish mottled markings on their upper surfaces. Alternating with these are three smaller, more erect, petals, within which there are three more yellow petal-like stigmas. These stigmas are curved and their curves conceal the stamens beneath. Flowering May to July.

Ribwort Plantain

RIBWORT PLANTAIN

Growing in moist shady woods and hedgerows, this perennial is formed from a red calyx with pinkish petals. The flower heads are carried in twos and threes on short stalks that sprout from long hairy stems.
The ovary of the flowers develop into capsules which when ripe spill their seed.
Flowering June to September.

COMMON TOADFLAX   *Linaria vulgaris*

Pick a flower and lay it on its back and you will notice a remarkable resemblance to a young frog emerging from the tadpole stage, including a small tail. This is how this quaint wild flower gets its name. The American name Brideweed is not easy to justify, although it is sometimes called Flaxweed and the spring time resemblance to a flax plant accounts for this name.
It is found near hedges in fields and waste-places and is perennial. Its rootstock is creeping. Its stems and leaves are a fine bluish-green and grow to 30cm. or 60cm. high.

Common Toadflax

White Campion

WHITE CAMPION

Silene vulgaris

Sometimes referred to as the Bladder Campion, a rather unattractive name for such an interesting flower. The name is derived from the sepals which are joined to form a greenish calyx, which has a darkly veined surface and which is said to resemble a bladder.

The white flowers are drooping and form terminal panicles. Each of the five petals are divided into two parts. There are ten stamens and anything from three to five styles.

It prefers a dry light soil.

Flowering June to September.

LADY'S SMOCK

Cardamine pratensis

Preferring a moist grassy terrain, the Lady's Smock has large flowers of a pale lilac colour, which are supported on erect stems which rise from the short rootstock. Propagation is from seeds which are ejected from the ripe slender seed pods, and also from rooting of the leaves. These roots appear at the axils of each leaflet, where they are in contact with suitable moist ground.

The leaves which rise from the rootstock are composed of a number of rounded leaflets, whereas the stem leaves are pinnate.

Flowering March to June.

Lady's Smock

Common Field Poppy

COMMON FIELD POPPY

Papaver rhoeas

Contrary to popular belief opium is not made from the Common Poppy, but from the juice of the Opium Poppy *(Papaver somniferum)*. The Common Poppy also exudes white juice from bruised stems and leaves, and this juice is particularly heavy in the flower heads and seed capsules. It has a heavy odour, and is commonly seen growing in fields of corn. The 60cm. stalks are covered with rough hairs and the flower heads are divided into four large petals. In the centre cup formed by the petals is a circle of stamens which shed their pollen into the centre, from where it is sought by insects. After the petals have fallen, the seed pods dry out and crack open, the seeds are then shaken out as the heads sway in the breeze. This thorough seeding action explains why poppies seed themselves so thoroughly and so quickly.

CORNFLOWER

Centaurea cyanus

Often found growing with Poppies among the corn, hence its common name Cornflower. The brilliance of its blue is so noteworthy that Cornflower blue as a colour is very well-known.

Its single blooms are carried on long hard stalks about 60cm. high, from the lower part of which spring the long deeply-lobed leaves. Higher up the tough stems the leaves are narrow and more plain in outline. Each flower bloom is a gathering of little flowers. The head consists of outer empty florets and inner fertile florets. These inner florets contain five stamens which form a tunnel through which the ovary column runs, and into which the pollen is poured. The end of the column is forked and has a ring of fine small hairs which form a small circular brush.

The stamens are sensitive to the touch of insects and when touched they contract, drawing the walls of the tunnel downwards and forcing the pollen out of the top with the hair brush.

Bristly Ox-Tongue

BRISTLY OX-TONGUE

Picris echiodes

The common name origin is apparent when one sets eyes on this plant. The whole is covered with coarse hairs which sprout from the leaves as well as the stalks. It can be annual or biennial and carries a golden yellow flowerhead composed of strap-shaped florets. These heads are soon replaced by heads of white silky hairs resembling the Dandelion seed heads. Its leaves are lanceolate and are carried on stalks where they rise from the rootstock, but the stem leaves are stalkless.

Flowering June to September.

CHICORY

Cichorium intybus

A chalky dry soil favours the growth of the perennial Chicory. The hairy stems rise from a fleshy rootstock and sport radical leaves that form a ground rosette and become sparse higher up the stem. The pale blue flowers are formed of two circular rows of bracts, the inner row being a little shorter than the outer.

The root of the plant is a constituent in certain blends of coffee, and the plant is cultivated with this in mind.

Flowering June to October.

Chicory

YARROW

Achillea millefolium

The Yarrow is a common wild flower and its strength enables it to survive where others would die. Although at first glance a rather unattractive plant, on close inspection one can appreciate the beauty of the tiny flowers that make up each little cluster of flower heads. The centre of the flowers are composed of several tubular corollas, the mouths of which are filled with five joined stamen heads. In mature florets a rod from the ovary below pushes itself through the stamens and opens into a fork. In so doing it pushes out the pollen, which falls and fertilises the flowers below.

The stems are often pale grey and finely furrowed, and rise from a creeping rootstock.

Flowering May to September.

RAGWORT

Senecio jacobaea

The tough root of the Ragwort forces its way into the toughest ground and makes the plant a common sight on waste-ground. Bright yellow flowers form a terminal corymb at the extremities of the branched stems. The leaves are divided into many lobes that give them a ragged appearance.

Yarrow

Ragwort

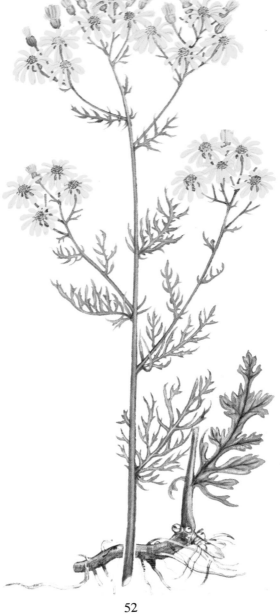

Knapweed

KNAPWEED

Centaurea nigra

The Knapweed is a very tough looking customer, having sinewy stems and branches and rough stalkless leaves. The name is a corruption of 'Knopweed', 'Knop' being an old English word for a knob or hard round globe. An investigation of a knop reveals overlapping scales like those of an armadillo. The Knapweed belongs to the same family as the Dandelion and Daisy, and yet its flower head is prettier, with a certain delicacy which is lacking in the other two. This prettiness is partly due to the effect of five elongated teeth on the petals which tend to make the flower head appear more supple. Inside the central florets are five stamens, the heads of which join to form a ring around a central shorter style. The pollen falls from the anthers into the small circular chamber formed by the anthers' walls. These walls are sensitive to touch by insects and can react, leaving the pollen exposed on the central style. This rather peculiar method of presenting the pollen to the insect as it arrives prevents the possibility of it being washed away by rain if it were continuously exposed. The stigmas of the adjacent flowers are fertilised by the insects and any that are overlooked will later curl back and fertilise themselves from pollen lying among the hairs below.
Average height 12cm. to 1m.

CREEPING THISTLE

Cirsium arvense

This robust perennial has branched erect, glabrous and grooved stems which grow from a creeping root. It is found in fields and on waste-ground. The lanceolate leaves have prickly margins. Its flowers are formed in loose terminal corymbs, and appear during May and June.

Creeping Thistle

Charlock or
Wild Mustard

CHARLOCK or **WILD MUSTARD**   *Sinapis arvensis*

This pretty yellow flower prefers a light dry soil and can be
seen in fields during the summer months.
The leaves are large and have saw-toothed edges and are
carried on stems rising to 50cm. high. The dark brown seeds
are carried in a pod in a single row, and these are often eaten
by birds.
Flowering May to August.

DANDELION   *Taraxacum officinale*

The margins of the Dandelion's leaves form jagged teeth,
and from this resemblance to lions' teeth the common name
originates *(Dent de Lion)*.
The bright yellow flower heads are sensitive to lighting variations and when rain threatens the heads close up. This
occurs again as night falls. The blooms are protected by
narrow green bracts which prevent unwanted insects from
crawling up the stem and damaging the flower heads.
In our illustration the left-hand stem shows the fully deve-
loped flower head, while the second stem shows the beautiful
gossamer ball of seeds which are carried on their fine 'para-
chutes' that gently float away on the lightest breeze. The
third stem shows the transition stage after the petals have
fallen and the seed pod is beginning to open out.
The leaves grow thickly and were it not for their intriguing
design, would cause the root to be shielded from the rain.
Each leaf however has a central groove, down which rain-
drops are channelled directly to the rootstock.
Flowering throughout the year.

Dandelion

Corn Sowthistle

CORN SOWTHISTLE

Sonchus arvensis

This perennial prefers a loose soil and may be found in cultivated fields.
The stems are long and hairy and grow to 1m. or 1½m. high.
They carry the toothed leaves which have no stalks, except at
the lower end of the stem. The attractive flower head consists
of a large number of ray florets, and emerges from a broad
hairy involucre.
Flowering August and September.

HARE-BELL

Campanula rotundifolia

The 'Bluebell of Scotland' as it is sometimes called prefers
hilly ground and heaths. The bell-shaped flowers often droop
and are formed by a corolla with five lobes, five stamens and
a style with three to five stigmas. The sinewy stems carry
broad heart-shaped leaves near the ground and thinner
leaves that become smaller and more slender as they near the
top of the stems. The stems are thin and flimsy and issue
from a creeping rootstock that assists the plant in its propagation. The ovary of the Hare-bell develops into a hard brown
capsule with thick ribs that contains many seeds.
Average height 15cm., trailing with rising stems to 50cm.
Flowers June to November.

Hare-bell

Field Scabious

FIELD SCABIOUS   *Knautia scorpioides*

This perennial herb has a tough penetrating root and favours a dry soil. It is often found in pastures and on chalky banks. The lanceolate leaves have toothed edges and form a rosette around the base of the straight hairy stems, which rise to a height of 60cm. or 1m.

The flower heads are composed of a large number of florets, massed together with the largest on the outside and reducing in size towards the centre. These vary in colour from a pale blue on the outside tending towards mauve in the centre. In some blooms the florets are imperfect, having neither anthers or pollen and only a rudimentary growth where the stamens should be.

The anthers being only lightly attached often drop before the petals. After the petals have dropped the green calyx at the flower base grows a number of long erect points, replacing the bloom with a globular bristling head composed of oval seed cases, each containing a single seed.

Flowers June to September.

BINDWEED   *Convolvulus arvensis*

The delicate creeping stems with their attractive bell-shaped flowers grow very quickly, with the result that this plant has become a pest in both Britain and North America. It winds itself around fence posts and around growing plants and its extensive roots make it difficult to eradicate completely. It is found growing wild in most countries of the World with the exception of the far northern countries.

The roots have been used for medicinal purposes. It is a perennial plant, found in hedgerows and woods.

Flowers June to September.

Bindweed

Wood Sorrel

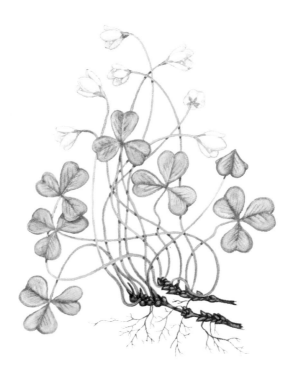

WOOD SORREL   *Oxalis acetosella*

Another lover of moist shady ground, the little Wood Sorrel can be found growing in great profusion in favourable conditions. The creeping tangled stems rise from a creeping rootstock, and where the stems touch the ground, fine roots sprout out. The light green delicate leaves are each composed of three heart-shaped leaflets which are coloured purple on their undersides. These leaflets are sensitive to light and are only fully extended when in shady conditions; should the sun strike them, they immediately sink down on to the stem to form a three-sided pyramid. At night or in dull overcast conditions they react rather differently, each leaflet folding itself downwards along the central rib.

The single blooms are white, tinged with pink and rise on stems directly from the rootstock. They are composed of five sepals, five petals, ten stamens and five stigmas.

The seeds are carried in capsules containing five cells formed around a central column in each of which are two seeds. When ripe the pod suddenly turns inside out and the seeds are ejected with considerable force.

Flowering April, May.

WILD DAFFODIL   *Narcissus pseudo-narcissus*

The Wild Daffodil grows from a bulbous rootstock from which linear leaves sprout. The single blooms are supported on a leafless stalk. The flower is formed from a ring of floral leaves, both sepals and petals being merged in it. There are six tall stamens. The seeds are contained in a capsule which when ripe splits open at the top. Propagation however is by multiplication of the bulbs.

Flowering March and April.

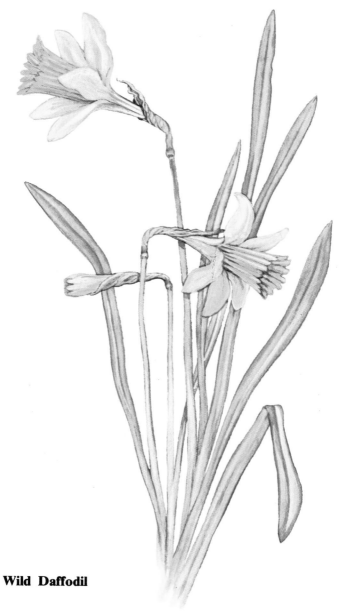

Wild Daffodil

HEATHER

Calluna vulgaris

Heather normally grows on heath and moorland and prefers an acid soil. It is an evergreen shrub which can grow to a considerable height. Its stems are wiry and straggling. The leaves are dark green and triangular, but very small and overlay each other in four rows along the branches. The mauve coloured flowers are carried in terminal spikes between July and September; very occasionally they are white.

BIRDS' FOOT TREFOIL

Lotus corniculatus

Growing wild in sandy or chalky soil, these tiny light yellow flowers can be found. The flowers are produced in mid-summer and are carried on long slim stems up to 50cm. long and are produced in small groups. The fruits give the flower its common name since they consist of thin, curved, split pods that give the appearance of a bird's foot.

WILD PEA

Lathyrus sylvestris

This is a glabrous perennial with a creeping rootstock and straggling or climbing stems. It grows from 1½m. to 2m. high and carries large reddish-purple flowers. Often found growing in hedgerows, woods and shady locations.
Flowering July and August.

Heather

Birds' Foot Trefoil

70

Wild Pea

Wild Strawberry

WILD STRAWBERRY

Fragaria vesca

The Wild Strawberry is a perennial herb which propagates via rooting runners of considerable length, which spring from a woody rootstock. It prefers a neutral soil and is found in woods and shady hedgerows.

The pretty white flowers are quite small and carried on stalks about 20cm. long. The leaves are hairy and are carried on long stalks and are composed of three oblong serrated leaflets.

Flowers June to August.

CREEPING CINQUEFOIL *Potentilla reptans*

At the sides of the highway and on grasslands may be found the small golden yellow flowers of the Creeping Cinquefoil. The solitary flowers rise on long stems from the axils of the leaves. There are five petals, each separated by the green sepals.

The rootstock is usually very long and branched at the top to form several crowns from which run stems of considerable length, which trail about, rooting at intervals, and which carry the long stalks which culminate in serrated palmate leaves.

Flowering June to September.

Creeping Cinquefoil

Common Mallow

75

COMMON MALLOW

Malva sylvestris

This plant is biennial or perennial and has a 1m. to 1½m. hairy stem, with lobed, roundish leaves, the margins of which have toothed edges. From the axils of the leaves grow the short stalks which carry the attractive lilac flowers, whose five petals are marked with fine darker lines radiating from their centres. Commonly found in open woodland.
Flowering July and August.

GERMANDER SPEEDWELL

Veronica chamaedrys

This perennial plant grows profusely and can be found in hedgerows and cultivated ground. It produces small blue flowers with white centres in paired racemes. The flower corolla is tubular, spreading at its top to four lobes, two of which are longer than the lateral pair. There are two stamens which are attached within the corolla tube from which the anthers and the stigma also protrude. The leaves are similar in appearance to small oak leaves. The minute ovary at the base of the stigma is divided into two cells each of which contain several seeds. It matures into a flattish capsule which when ripe splits at the edges to spread the seed. The stems are rather interesting and carry two lines of long hairs which run down between each pair of leaves and form a natural barrier against unwanted crawling insects. Its leaves are arranged in pairs alternating one with another. They have serrated edges, and are rough and hairy. There are some sixteen species of Speedwell, some of which have white or pinkish flowers instead of the common blue variety.
Flowering May to June.

Germander Speedwell

TANSY

Chrysanthemum vulgare

This perennial is found at the roadside and on waste-places. It is a stout plant and has a pungent odour. Its broad fern-like leaves rise from a creeping rootstock and grow to a height of 60cm. or 1m. The golden yellow flower heads are enclosed in a half rounded involucre of tough bracts.
Flowering August to September.

VIPER'S BUGLOSS

Echium vulgare

Favouring a light dry soil and a sunny position it is usually to be found in grassy meadows. The lanceolate leaves sprout directly from strong, erect stems which grow to a height of 60cm. or 1m. The blue corolla is tube-shaped and has five stamens, one of which is much shorter and is hidden within the tube. Later, another column grows out beyond them. Originating in the ovary, and clothed with tiny hairs, its end is forked into two branches, which helps in the cross-fertilisation of the flowers.
The flowers are covered with a coating of soft fine hairs, while on the stems sharp and stiffer hairs each sprout from single dark glands.
It was first introduced into America in 1683, and soon took a firm hold as an unwanted weed. Around 1830 Dr. Asa Gray the naturalist reported that it had overrun one hundred square miles of a certain valley in Virginia.
Flowering August.

Tansy

Viper's Bugloss

Common Forget-me-not

COMMON FORGET-ME-NOT
Myosotis arvensis

There are several species of this plant, the commonest, a perennial, grows from a creeping rootstock beside streams and in other damp localities.

The leaves are long and narrow and are covered with tiny hairs which are inclined towards the leaf tip, making it difficult for insects to crawl towards the stem.

The flowers are light blue with a yellow centre and contain five stamens and a short style which are hidden in the tubular base of the corolla. These flowers are grouped in cymes, on a thick smooth stem, which rises from a creeping rootstock which also gives off many runners.

Flowering May to July.

PERFORATE ST. JOHN'S WORT
Hypericum perforatum

There are several different species of this plant with minor variations. This variety has a soft hairy coat on its stem and along the veins on the undersides of the leaves. The leaves have short stalks and are covered with translucent spots. These spots are in fact small glands which contain an oily aromatic fluid scent.

The individual flowers which make up the flower cluster have a large number of golden stamens of differing lengths gathered in groups. There are five green sepals forming a protective cup and these are edged with small glands which appear as conspicuous dark dots. The five narrow petals are about double the length of the sepals and radiate out behind the stamen groups.

Flowering June to October.

Perforate St. John's Wort

RED CAMPION   *Silene dioica*

The Red Campion is similar to the White Campion but
differs in its seed capsules which are egg-shaped and develop
from the ovary. This splits at its narrower end, spilling the
small seeds.
Frequents moist, shady woods and hedgerows. It is to be
found all through the summer.
Perennial. Average height 30cm. to 1m.

CREEPING BUTTERCUP   *Ranunculus repens*

This stout perennial has a creeping rootstock, out of which
grow grooved stems up to a height of 20cm. The stems are
branched and these branches carry the hairy leaves at their
apex. The leaves are attractively lobed and are deeply cut.
It is an abundant plant found in meadows, hedgerows, fields,
riverbanks and waste-places.

Red Campion

Creeping Buttercup

White Dead-Nettle

Bugle

WHITE DEAD-NETTLE *Lamium album*

Found under hedges, on banks and on waste-ground, this plant is allied to the Coleus. It is perennial and has an average height of only 15cm., trailing with rising square stems which grow up to 20cm. high. The rootstock is creeping. The White Dead-Nettle does not sting.
Flowering May to August.

BUGLE *Ajuga reptans*

This perennial herb, which is to be found in damp places, has blue flowers which are carried on the upper part of erect square stems which emanate from a thick and strong creeping rootstock. The flowers form elongated inflorescences which spring from the axils of the leaves, which are ovate and borne in pairs.
Flowering June to September.

Ox-eye Daisy

OX-EYE DAISY
Chrysanthemum leucanthemum

A common sight in fields and pasture, the Ox-eye Daisy stands erect on 30cm. high stems, from which sprout radical leaves. The bloom is composed of a series of overlapping scales with brown edges, the ray florets are white and the disc florets a golden yellow.
Flowers May to August.

DOG ROSE
Rosa canina

Many varieties of the Dog Rose exist, and it is among the commonest of wild roses. The strong stems carry flowers in small clusters, each with five green sepals, five pink petals and numerous stamens. The leaves are pinnate and have two or three pairs of ovate serrated leaflets.
Flowering June and July.

SCENTLESS CHAMOMILE
Matricaria inodora

This annual plant is low spreading and sends up long straight branches with alternate leaves. It is to be found in fields and waste-places throughout the seasons.
The single blooms are carried on long stalks, the involucre consisting of overlapping bracts. The yellow central disc florets contain both anthers and pistil whilst the white ray florets contains pistils only.
Flowering May to July.

Dog Rose

Scentless Chamomile

A Glossary of Botanical Terms
used in the Text

Achene: A small dry fruit, formed from a single carpel and containing a single seed.

Alternate: Leaves growing at different levels along a stem.

Anther: The swollen end of a stamen, containing the pollen.

Berry: A fleshy fruit containing many seeds.

Bract: A small leaf borne on a stem, often beneath the flower.

Calyx: The outer whorl of the flower, the sepals.

Capitulum: A compact inflorescence of tiny flowers on a flat or convex base, e.g. Dandelion.

Carpel: Part of the female part of the flower which produces ovules.

Corolla: The inner whorl of the flower, the petals.

Cyme: An inflorescence in which the apex is crowned by a flower with further flowers on laterals below.

Disc floret: The small central tubular flowers, e.g. in Coltsfoot.

Floret: A small flower, applied usually to one of a large number in an inflorescence.

Follicle: A dry fruit formed from a single carpel, containing seeds later shed from a split along one side of the wall.

Glabrous: Smooth, without hair or down.

Inflorescence: A group of flowers, including the stems on which they are carried.

Involucre: A group of bracts surrounding a capitulum.

Node: A sort of knot on the stem where a leaf is attached.

Opposite: Where two leaves are inserted in either side of the same node.

Ovary: The hollow basal part of a carpel, containing one or more ovules.

Ovule: A part within the ovary which after fertilisation becomes the seed.

Palmate: A compound leaf with the leaflets attached to the end of the leaf stalk, in the shape of a hand.

Pinnate: A compound leaf with the leaflets arranged in two lateral rows.

Pollen: Microscopic grains produced in the anthers, which fertilise the ovules.

Raceme: A type of inflorescence in which a number of flowers with short and equal stalks stand on a common slender axis, e.g. currant.

Radical: Leaves which sprout at ground level, often forming a rosette.

Ray floret: The small outer flowers of a capitulum, with strap-shaped florets.

Rhizome: A horizontal penetrating underground stem.

Stamen: One of the units of the male part of the flower which produces pollen.

Stigma: The upper extremity of the style and the part which in impregnation receives the pollen.

Style: A part of the prolongation of the top of the ovary (the carpel) which supports the stigma.

Terminal: A flower carried at the end of a stem, thereby preventing further growth.

Umbel: An inflorescence in which all flower stalks, nearly equal in length, arise from one point at the end of the main stalk.

Index

TYPES OF SHOOT

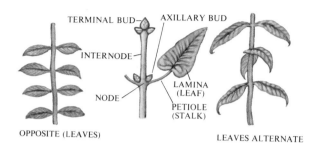

TERMINAL BUD — AXILLARY BUD

INTERNODE

NODE

LAMINA (LEAF)

PETIOLE (STALK)

OPPOSITE (LEAVES)

LEAVES ALTERNATE

TYPES OF ROOT

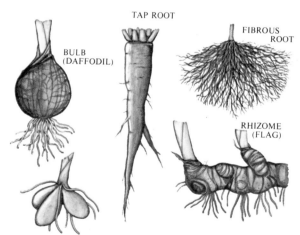

TAP ROOT

FIBROUS ROOT

BULB (DAFFODIL)

RHIZOME (FLAG)

ROOT TUBERS (LESSER CELANDINE)

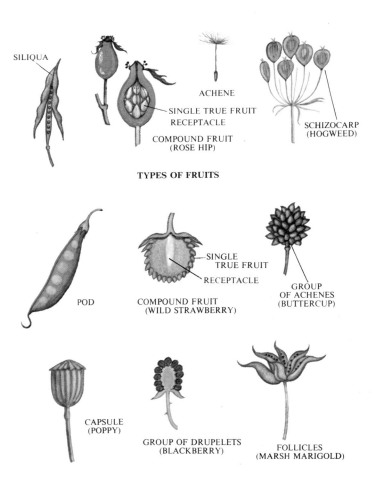

SILIQUA

ACHENE

SINGLE TRUE FRUIT

RECEPTACLE

COMPOUND FRUIT
(ROSE HIP)

SCHIZOCARP
(HOGWEED)

TYPES OF FRUITS

POD

SINGLE
TRUE FRUIT

RECEPTACLE

COMPOUND FRUIT
(WILD STRAWBERRY)

GROUP
OF ACHENES
(BUTTERCUP)

CAPSULE
(POPPY)

GROUP OF DRUPELETS
(BLACKBERRY)

FOLLICLES
(MARSH MARIGOLD)

TYPES OF LEAVES

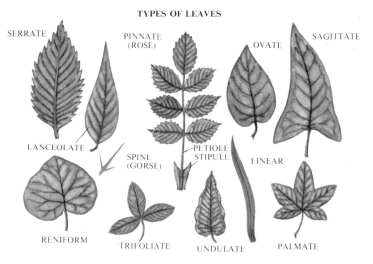

SERRATE

PINNATE
(ROSE)

OVATE

SAGITTATE

LANCEOLATE

SPINE
(GORSE)

PETIOLE
STIPULE

LINEAR

RENIFORM

TRIFOLIATE

UNDULATE

PALMATE

TYPES OF STEMS

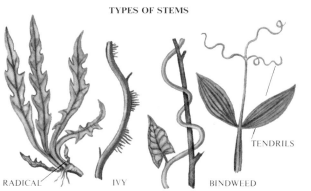

RADICAL

IVY

BINDWEED

TENDRILS

TYPES OF INFLORESCENCES

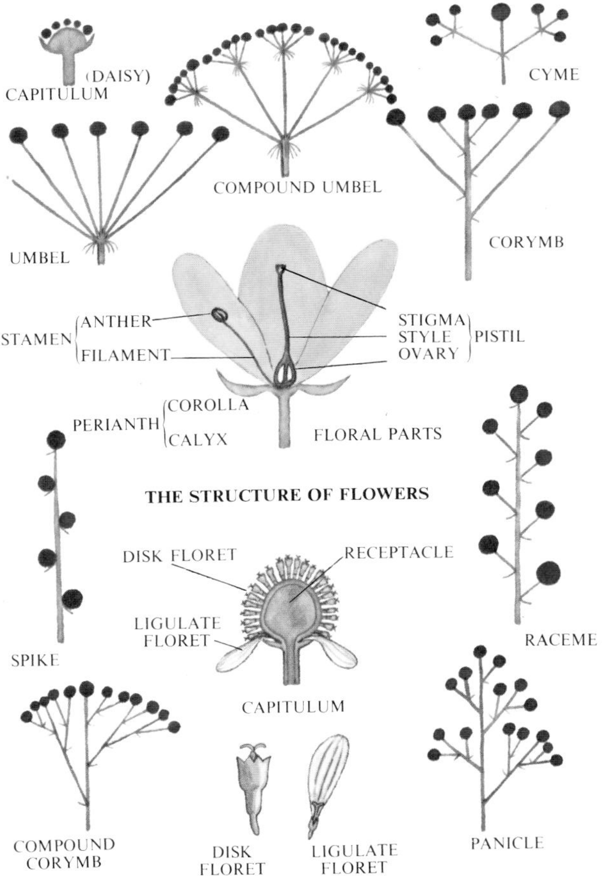

CAPITULUM (DAISY)

CYME

COMPOUND UMBEL

UMBEL

CORYMB

STAMEN { ANTHER
FILAMENT }

STIGMA
STYLE } PISTIL
OVARY

PERIANTH { COROLLA
CALYX }

FLORAL PARTS

THE STRUCTURE OF FLOWERS

SPIKE

DISK FLORET

RECEPTACLE

LIGULATE FLORET

RACEME

CAPITULUM

COMPOUND CORYMB

DISK FLORET

LIGULATE FLORET

PANICLE